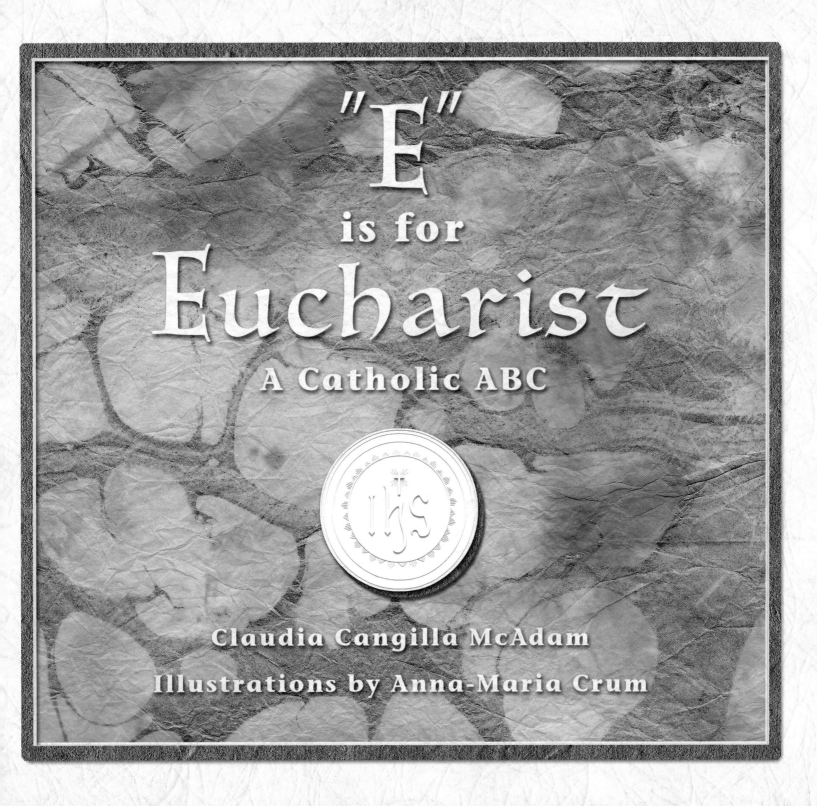

"E"
is for
Eucharist
A Catholic ABC

Claudia Cangilla McAdam

Illustrations by Anna-Maria Crum

Dedication

With love for my grandson Finnean,
whose beautiful faith strengthens my own —C.C.M.

With thanks to Claudia, whose friendship and faith
are an inspiration —A.L.C.

Illustrations by Anna-Maria Crum

ISBN: 978-1-5051-1750-9
Kindle ISBN: 978-1-5051-1751-6
ePUB ISBN: 978-1-5051-1752-3

Published in the United States by
TAN Books
PO Box 269
Gastonia, NC 28053
www.TANBooks.com

ur Catholic faith is a cherished gift,
Given by Jesus to you and me.
Rich in beliefs, traditions, and truths,
So many treasures from A to Z!

shes   At Lent, they're smudged upon your head

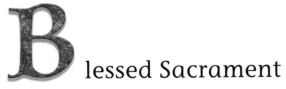 lessed Sacrament   The Body of the Lord, once bread

rucifix — The cross on which our Savior died

eacon

Ordained to serve at Father's side

E ucharist

A sacred feast; thanksgiving meal

asting   To give up things with great appeal

 enuflect

To honor God on bended knee

 oly Spirit

Third Person of the Trinity

ncense   Sweet scents lift pleas to God above

esus

Redeemer King who died for love

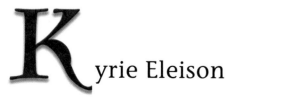yrie Eleison　　　　Means "Lord have mercy" in the Greek

 iturgy

Works of worship and words we speak

ary Christ's mother, pure and free from sin

arthex

Church entry space; it's just within

riginal Sin

First parents' failure marks us all

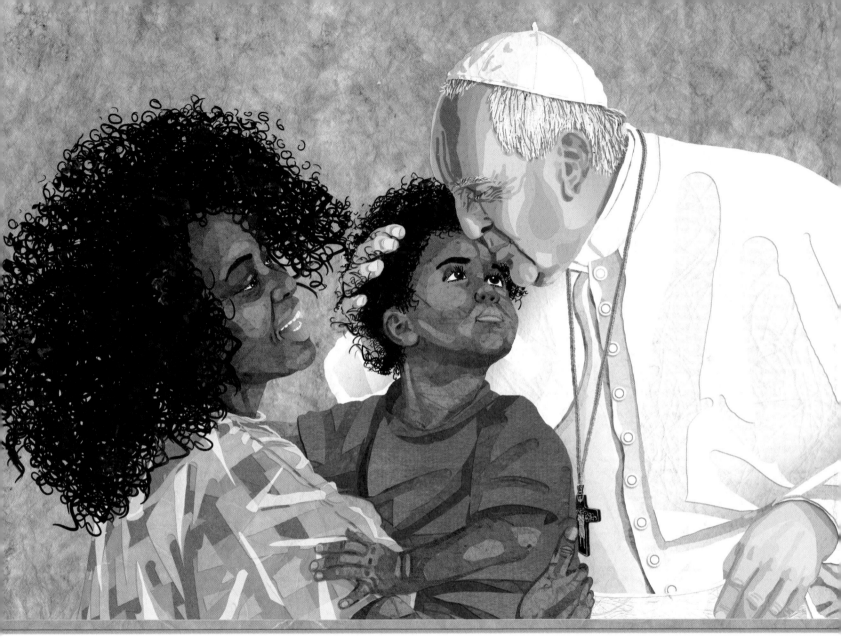

ope   Church leader who hears Spirit's call

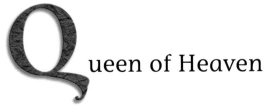 ueen of Heaven   Our Blessed Mother's royal name

osary

Beaded prayers that we proclaim

Sacraments   Outward signs of inward grace

 abernacle　　　　　　Eucharistic dwelling place

Universal

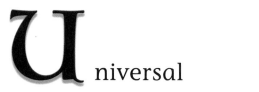

This word explains what "Catholic" means

estments Priests' robes in reds, whites, purples, greens

Wine

The blood of Jesus, sacrificed

Χριστός

First letter of Greek word for "Christ"

 ahweh   God's holy name, from way back when

ucchetto

A round cap worn by clergymen

What Jesus taught came down to us
From Apostles, through the ages.
Thank you, God, for our Catholic faith,
We pray as we close these pages.

Author's Note:

Claudia Cangilla McAdam is an award-winning children's author and a lifelong Catholic. She has penned two dozen books, most of them for youth. Claudia holds a master's degree in theology, and her works invite young readers and their families to explore the beauty of the faith. *"E" is for Eucharist* is her second alphabet book. The first was about the state of Colorado, where she and her husband live not far from their children and grandchildren.

For a free Discussion and Activities Guide for *"E" is for Eucharist*, visit www.ClaudiaMcAdam.com. You'll find fun stuff to do, you can investigate more "Catholic things" for various letters, and you'll learn additional bits of information about the items included in this book. For example, did you know that priests' vestments come in more than the four colors listed on the "V" page?

If you look closely, you'll find one of the illustrations in this book shows vestments in the color "rose." That color is only worn on two days during the whole year. Do you know which days those are? What does that color symbolize? Those answers are in the Discussion and Activities Guide!

Illustrator's Note:

Anna-Maria Crum started writing and illustrating her stories when she was seven years old. Today she's an award-winning illustrator and the author of 22 grade school readers.

The illustrations in this book were done using a new technique she calls "digital cut-paper." Anna-Maria carefully selects handmade art papers for their color and texture. She scans the papers into the computer and then creates shapes using the selected papers in Adobe Photoshop and Illustrator. She further enhances the illusion of depth by adding cast shadows and layer masks.

One of the illustrations in this book has almost 600 layers! Can you guess which one it is? For the answer, go to www.annamariacrum.com. There is also a downloadable activity sheet there where kids can assemble their own artwork using a type of paper collage reminiscent of the ones in this book.